Compiled by
ROSALIE MAGGIO

Quotations
FOR THE *Soul*

PRENTICE HALL
Paramus, New Jersey 07652

Library of Congress Cataloging-in-Publication Data

Quotations for the soul / compiled by Rosalie Maggio
    p. cm.
   ISBN 0-13-769159-9
    1. Religion—Quotations, maxims, etc. 2. Spirituality—
Quotations, maxims, etc. I. Maggio, Rosalie.
PN6084.R3Q68 1997
200—dc21   97-35714
                    CIP

ISBN 0-13-769159-9

Excerpts from *The New Beacon Book of Quotations by Women* (Boston: Beacon Press, 1996) are reprinted with permission.

PRENTICE HALL
Career & Personal Development
Paramus, NJ 07652
A Simon & Schuster Company

On the World Wide Web at http://www.phdirect.com

Prentice Hall International (UK) Limited, *London*
Prentice Hall of Australia Pty. Limited, *Sydney*
Prentice Hall Canada, Inc., *Toronto*
Prentice Hall Hispanoamericana, S.A., *Mexico*
Prentice Hall of India Private Limited, *New Delhi*
Prentice Hall of Japan, Inc., *Tokyo*
Simon & Schuster Asia Pte. Ltd., *Singapore*
Editora Prentice Hall do Brasil, Ltda., *Rio de Janeiro*

All the way to heaven is heaven.

St. Catherine of Siena

To Katie

$\mathscr{C}$ONTENTS

$\mathcal{I}$NTRODUCTION

In the United States today, we seem to be concerned with our souls in unprecedented numbers and in new and diverse ways. The flourishing spiritual bouquet includes traditional domesticated blooms as well as surprising hybrids and sturdy wildflowers. New reflections on the nature of spiritual things, on our own souls, and on what it means to be both divinely human and humanly divine are joining and sometimes replacing more codified beliefs. Organized religions have much to offer us, but we've discovered that ultimately we are responsible for our own souls. We thus find ourselves reinventing the wheel, but it is a wheel of our own making, and we like this.

Almost every topic I can think of (with the exception perhaps of cigarettes and oysters) has a spiritual dimension. No, I take that back. I can see some spiritual dimensions in cigarettes and oysters. But one can't include everything so I had to make choices in compiling this collection. Some themes and ideas are fairly standard: the existence of the soul; the presence of a God (or Higher Power or Creator); the nearly universal hunger for something bigger than, yet paradoxically within, ourselves. Other themes that felt important to me were that there are as many ways of being spiritual as there are people who want to be spiritual; that a grateful heart is not only good for our mental health but is an indispensable part of spiritual well-being; that the ordinary is holy.

Just as you will notice the use of the outdated "thee" and "thou" in several quotations, you will notice some sexist language (for example, "If a man will begin with certainties, he shall end in doubts . . ." instead of "If you will begin with certainties, you shall end in doubts . . ."). Out of respect for those quoted, I have left all language as it was originally written or translated. However, I hope you will notice the exclusion of women and mentally or physically write them back in.

In many of the quotations, God is referred to as male. Although we have not assigned God a sexual orientation, a height, or eye color, we have thought nothing of assigning a gender and a religion (God always belongs to the same one we do). Theologians have never said God was male; on the contrary, they have always maintained that God is pure spirit. In the fourth century, Gregory of Nazianzus said that "Father" and "Son" did not name God's nature or essence but rather were metaphors to make Spirit accessible to us. Sandra M. Schneiders lists some of the metaphors we have for God (sun, rock, fire, lion, she-bear, mother eagle, potter, builder, shepherd, midwife, judge, king, mother, husband, father) and says, "While we are immediately aware that the personal God is not really a rock or a mother eagle, it is easy enough to imagine that God is really a king or a father. . . . We create the metaphor to say something about God; but then God seems to be saying something about the vehicle of the metaphor. Thus, if God is a king, there is a tendency to see kings as divine. If God is male, then males are divine and masculinity becomes normative of humanity."

In time I expect that we will expand our ideas of God so that we can all find the metaphors that best support a living relationship with the Holy. Until then, appreciate the thoughts and recognize that each writer is seeing God from a personal angle.

This book is dedicated to a woman who honors her soul, a soul fierce with authenticity and courage. Visionary, playful, discerning, and loving, she shares her talents, warmth, money, and time. It is no accident that she murmurs, "I hear you" when speaking with you. She has a gift for hearing—sounds of the real world and sounds too high for human ears. For her, as for George Eliot, "The world is full of hopeful analogies and handsome, dubious eggs, called possibilities." She waits in joyful expectation—of everything.

THE SPIRITUAL

After decades of declining influence on the affairs of the world, there is once again a widespread consideration of spiritual principles as an antidote to the pain of our times.

MARIANNE WILLIAMSON

Life is really about a spiritual unfolding that is personal and enchanting—an unfolding that no science or philosophy or religion has yet fully clarified.

JAMES REDFIELD

The soul needs an intense, full-bodied spiritual life as much as and in the same way that the body needs food.

THOMAS MOORE

Sooner or later there arises in every human heart
the desire for holiness, spirituality, God, call it what
you will.

ANTHONY DE MELLO

Among all my patients in the second half of life—
that is to say over thirty-five—there has not been one
whose problem in the last resort was not that of finding a religious outlook on life.

CARL JUNG

Being religious means asking passionately the question of the meaning of our existence and being will-
ing to receive answers, even if the answers hurt.

PAUL TILLICH

The longest journey is the journey inward.

DAG HAMMARSKJÖLD

There is only one journey. Going inside yourself.

RAINER MARIA RILKE

If we go down into ourselves we find that we possess exactly what we desire.

SIMONE WEIL

If you do not go within, you go without.

NEALE DONALD WALSCH

The externals are simply so many props; everything we need is within us.

ETTY HILLESUM

O God
why do I storm heaven
for answers
that are already in my heart?

MACRINA WIEDERKEHR

All you need is deep within you waiting to unfold
and reveal itself. All you have to do is be still and
take time to seek for what is within, and you will
surely find it.

EILEEN CADDY

Delve within; within is the fountain of good, and it
is always ready to bubble up, if you always delve.

MARCUS AURELIUS

There is a spiritual realm that is available to all who find its many entrances.

JAMES MELVIN WASHINGTON

No great spiritual event befalls those who do not summon it.

ELBERT HUBBARD

Spirituality is an inner fire, a mystical sustenance that feeds our souls. The mystical journey drives us into ourselves, to a sacred flame at our center. The purpose of the religious experience is to develop the eyes by which we see this inner flame, and our capacity to live its mystery. In its presence, we are warmed and ignited. When too far from the blaze, we are cold and spiritually lifeless. We are less than human without that heat. Our connection to God is life itself.

MARIANNE WILLIAMSON

My belief is that we did not come from God so much as that we are going towards God.

JANE DUNCAN

I am certainly convinced that it is one of the greatest impulses of mankind to arrive at something higher than a natural state.

JAMES BALDWIN

Spiritual life is like a moving sidewalk. Whether you go with it or spend your whole life running against it, you're still going to be taken along.

BERNADETTE ROBERTS

I don't know Who—or what—put the question, I don't know when it was put. I don't even remember answering. But at some moment I did answer *Yes* to Someone—or Something—and from that hour I was certain that existence is meaningful and that, therefore, my life, in self-surrender, had a goal.

DAG HAMMARSKJÖLD

Until you have found God in your own soul, the whole world will seem meaningless to you.

RABINDRANATH TAGORE

He who has a *why* to live for can bear almost any *how*.

FRIEDRICH NIETZSCHE

To be ordinary is not a choice:
It is the usual freedom
Of men without visions.

THOMAS MERTON

The spiritual life is a reaching out to our innermost self, to our fellow human beings and to our God.

HENRI J.M. NOUWEN

Spirituality is rooted in desire. We long for something we can neither name nor describe, but which is no less real because of our inability to capture it with words.

MARY JO WEAVER

The higher goal of spiritual living is not to amass a wealth of information, but to face sacred moments.

ABRAHAM JOSHUA HESCHEL

I have come to believe in the "Sacrament of the Moment," which presupposes trust in the ultimate goodness of my creator.

RUTH CASEY

Every time you don't follow your inner guidance, you feel a loss of energy, loss of power, a sense of spiritual deadness.

SHAKTI GAWAIN

Follow your bliss.

JOSEPH CAMPBELL

To be religious is to be sensitive to reality. Your total being—body, mind and heart—is sensitive to . . . everything about you.

KRISHNAMURTI

The spirituality of my childhood is the one I would most like to have restored. It was pure and fresh and honest. I read God everywhere!

MACRINA WIEDERKEHR

Spirituality is basically our relationship with reality.

CHANDRA PATEL

A conversion is the starting point of every spiritual journey.

GUSTAVO GUTIERREZ

Conversion means simply turning around.

VINCENT MCNABB

"Conversion," like "loving" or "education," is a continuing process; it cannot be shut off in isolated moments, or given a cut-and-dried definition.

MALCOLM BOYD

Have patience with everything unresolved in your heart and try to love *the questions themselves*. . . . Don't search for the answers, which could not be given to you now, because you would not be able to live them. And the point is, to live everything. *Live* the questions now. Perhaps, then, someday far in the future, you will gradually, without even noticing it, live your way into the answer.

RAINER MARIA RILKE

The first key to wisdom is assiduous and frequent questioning.... For by doubting we come to inquiry, and by inquiry we arrive at truth.

PETER ABELARD

If a man will begin with certainties, he shall end in doubts; but if he will be content to begin with doubts, he shall end in certainties.

FRANCIS BACON

Doubts are the messengers of the Living One to the honest. They are the first knock at our door of things that are not yet, but have to be, understood . . . . Doubts must precede every deeper assurance; for uncertainties are what we first see when we look into a region hitherto unknown, unexplored, unannexed.

GEORGE MACDONALD

The supernatural is only the natural of which the laws are not yet understood.

AGATHA CHRISTIE

We shall not cease from exploration
And the end of all our exploring
Will be to arrive where we started
And know the place for the first time.

T.S. ELIOT

What I ask for is absurd: that life shall have a meaning. What I strive for is impossible: that my life shall acquire a meaning. I dare not believe, I do not see how I shall ever be able to believe: that I am not alone.

DAG HAMMARSKJÖLD

Ask, and you will receive. Seek, and you will find. Knock, and it will be opened to you.

JESUS CHRIST

God's love is just like the sun, constant and shining for us all. And just as the earth rotates around the sun, it is the natural order for us to move away for a season, and then to return closer, but always within the appropriate time.

BETTY J. EADIE

Love is what we were born with. Fear is what we learned here. The spiritual journey is the relinquishment—or unlearning—of fear and the acceptance of love back into our hearts.

MARIANNE WILLIAMSON

It will cost something to be religious: it will cost more to be not so.

J. MASON

OD

In the beginning God . . . in the end God.

DESMOND TUTU

God is the East and the West, and wherever ye turn, there is God's face.

AL'QURAN

God is a circle whose center is everywhere and whose circumference is nowhere.

EMPEDOCLES

God is a sea of infinite substance.

ST. JOHN OF DAMASCUS

Let nothing disturb thee;
Let nothing dismay thee:
All things pass;
God never changes.

ST. TERESA OF AVILA

God is seated in the hearts of all.

THE BHAGAVAD-GITA

To think of God is not to find Him as an object in
our minds but to find ourselves in Him.

ABRAHAM JOSHUA HESCHEL

We shall discover God by encounter, but inside not outside ourselves. Inside not outside him.

CARLO CARRETTO

God is inside you and inside everybody else. You come into the world with God. But only them that search for it inside find it. And sometimes it just manifest itself even if you not looking, or don't know what you looking for. Trouble do it for most folks, I think . . . . Yeah, It. God ain't a he or a she, but a It.

ALICE WALKER

God is an unutterable sigh in the Human Heart, said the old German mystic. And therewith said the last word.

HAVELOCK ELLIS

The kingdom of God is within you.

JESUS CHRIST

God is being itself, not *a* being.

PAUL TILLICH

Whatever is, is in God.

BARUCH SPINOZA

There is no place to which we could flee from God which is outside God.

PAUL TILLICH

God is not
the voice in the whirlwind
god is the whirlwind.

MARGARET ATWOOD

God moves in a mysterious way
His wonders to perform;
He plants his footsteps in the sea
And rides upon the storm.

WILLIAM COWPER

Apprehend God in all things, for God is in all
things.

MEISTER ECKHART

He who sees Me everywhere, and sees everything in Me, I am not lost to him nor is he lost to Me.

THE BHAGAVAD-GITA

The highest condition of the religious sentiment is when . . . the worshiper not only sees God everywhere, but sees nothing which is not full of God.

HARRIET MARTINEAU

The world is charged with the grandeur of God.

GERARD MANLEY HOPKINS

God, I can push the grass apart
And lay my finger on Thy heart!

EDNA ST. VINCENT MILLAY

Earth's crammed with heaven,
And every common bush afire with God.

ELIZABETH BARRETT BROWNING

The heavens declare the glory of God; and the firmament showeth his handiwork.

PSALMS 19:2

Nature is too thin a screen; the glory of the omnipresent God bursts through everywhere.

RALPH WALDO EMERSON

This whole world is full of God!

BLESSED ANGELA OF FOLIGNO

All are but parts of one stupendous whole,
Whose body Nature is, and God the soul.

ALEXANDER POPE

The best way to know God is to love many things.

VINCENT VAN GOGH

God reveals herself through our relationships not
only to other people but also to other creatures and
nature.

CARTER HEYWARD

Every single creature is full of God and is a book
about God.

MEISTER ECKHART

You can never prove God; you can only find Him.

KATE DOUGLAS WIGGIN

Nature herself has imprinted on the minds of all the idea of a God.

CICERO

Whoever it was who searched the heavens with a telescope and found no God would not have found the human mind if he had searched the brain with a microscope.

GEORGE SANTAYANA

God will of necessity always be a hidden God. His loudest cry is silence. If he does not manifest himself to us, we will say that he hides himself. And if he manifests himself, we will accuse him of veiling himself. Ah! it is not easy for God to make himself known to us!

LOUIS EVELY

Our responding to life's unfairness with sympathy and with righteous indignation, God's compassion and God's anger working through us, may be the surest proof of all of God's reality.

HAROLD S. KUSHNER

I myself believe that the evidence for God lies primarily in inner personal experiences.

WILLIAM JAMES

God is rich in mercy. I know this wealth of his with the certainty of experience, I have touched it.

SIMONE WEIL

Whate'er we leave to God, God does
And blesses us.

HENRY DAVID THOREAU

If there be anywhere on earth a lover of God who is always kept safe from falling, I know nothing of it, for it was not shown me. But this was shown: that whether in falling or in rising we are always kept in the same precious love.

JULIAN OF NORWICH

We are all falling. Here, this hand falls.
And see—there goes another. It's in us all.
And yet there's One whose gently holding hands
let this falling fall and never land.

RAINER MARIA RILKE

In the center of all things is a Mighty Heart, which, having begotten all things, loves them; and, having born them into life, beats with great throbs of love towards them.

OLIVE SCHREINER

When one finds himself, one finds God. You find God and you find yourself.

THE ARTIST FORMERLY KNOWN AS PRINCE

i found god in myself
& i loved her
i loved her fiercely.

NTOZAKE SHANGE

I believe I have had a glimpse of God many times. I believe because believing is believable, and no one can prove it unbelievable.

DUKE ELLINGTON

If God is your target, you're in luck, because *God is so big, you can't miss.*

NEALE DONALD WALSCH

Why believe we'll realize God years from now, after many years of spiritual practice, after many more lifetimes of practice? She's right here, right now! We don't have to wait another second.

LINDA JOHNSEN

I believe in God, in the same way in which I believe in my friends, because I feel the breath of his love and his invisible, intangible hand, bringing me here, carrying me there, pressing upon me.

MIGUEL DE UNAMUNO Y JUGO

In all religiousness there lurks the suspicion that we invented the story that God loves us.

SEBASTIAN MOORE

I believe that God is in me as the sun is in the color and fragrance of a flower—the Light in my darkness, the Voice in my silence.

HELEN KELLER

If there were no God, it would be necessary to invent one.

FRANÇOIS M.A DE VOLTAIRE

My soul was always so full of aspirations, that a God was a necessity to me. I was like a bird with an instinct of migration upon me, and a country to migrate to was as essential as it is to the bird.

HANNAH WHITALL SMITH

Naught but God
Can satisfy the soul.

PHILIP JAMES BAILEY

You should not say, "God is in my heart," but
rather, "I am in the heart of God."

KAHLIL GIBRAN

The only thing that initially separates you from God
is the belief that you *are* separate.

RICHARD ROHR

God is the other within that ends an otherwise
ineluctable inner loneliness.

SEBASTIAN MOORE

God has always been to me not so much like a
father as like a dear and tender mother.

HARRIET BEECHER STOWE

The unfathomable mystery of God is that God is a
Lover who wants to be loved.

HENRI J.M. NOUWEN

God is our refuge and our strength, an ever-present
help in distress.

PSALMS 46:1

God is at home. It is we who have gone out for a
walk.

MEISTER ECKHART

God often visits us, but most of the time we are not at home.

JOSEPH ROUX

One way to express the spiritual crisis of our time is to say that most of us have an address but cannot be found there.

HENRI J.M. NOUWEN

Be still, and know that I am God.

PSALMS 46:10

He is the first and the last, the manifest and the hidden: and He knoweth all things.

AL'QURAN

All things change,—creeds and philosophies and outward systems,—but God remains!

Mrs. Humphry Ward

God does not ask anything else of you except that you let yourself go and let God be God in you.

Meister Eckhart

Be fervent in God, and let nothing grieve you, whatever you encounter.

Hadewijch

Far beyond your intellect, far beyond your understanding, lies inexhaustible knowledge and wealth, strength and power, peace and joy. Do not use your intellect to find the answers for God and his manifestations. Everything is God.

SWAMI VISHNU-DEVANANDA

"Let me understand that I may believe," say you. And I say, "Believe that you may understand."

ST. AUGUSTINE

God, so approachable by him who knows how to love, is hidden from him who knows only how to understand.

ALEXIS CARREL

God is not what you imagine or what you think you understand. If you understand you have failed.

St. Augustine

I know it does not matter
That I do not understand.

Brendan Kennelly

God is the one reality that cannot be defined.

Sebastian Moore

I know not which is the more childish—to deny God, or to define Him.

Samuel Butler

God cannot be grasped by the mind. If he could be grasped he would not be God.

EVAGRIUS PONTICUS

The less theorizing you do about God, the more receptive you are to his inpouring.

MEISTER ECKHART

It is easy to understand God as long as you don't try to explain Him.

JOSEPH JOUBERT

The knowledge of God is very far from the love of Him.

BLAISE PASCAL

God is always more unlike what we say than like it.

DENISE LARDNER CARMODY

Man pictures God like himself—the indulgent man worships an indulgent God, the stern man a stern God.

JOSEPH JOUBERT

If God has created us in his image, we have more than returned the compliment.

FRANÇOIS M.A DE VOLTAIRE

When we choose a god we choose one as much like ourselves as possible, or even more so!

REBECCA WEST

Many Christians wouldn't want the God
they've fabricated:
they'd be more likable than that!

Louis Evely

As truly as God is our Father, so truly is God our
Mother.

Julian of Norwich

We can know what God is not, but we cannot know
what He is.

St. Augustine

Nothing is stranger, more disconcerting, more misleading than a manifestation of God. We always take God to be different from what he is.

LOUIS EVELY

The way God has been thought of for thousands of years is no longer convincing; if anything is dead, it can only be the traditional *thought of God*.

HANNAH ARENDT

In some not altogether frivolous sense God needs to be liberated from our theology. Theology is not a tabernacle to contain the One who is Ahead, but it is a sign on the way, and thus is provisional.

JOAN ARNOLD ROMERO

Cast all your cares on God; that anchor holds.

ALFRED, LORD TENNYSON

Home is the definition of God.

EMILY DICKINSON

For the only air of the soul, in which it can breathe and live, is the presence of God and the spirits of the just: that is our heaven, our home, our all-right place.

GEORGE MACDONALD

The best name for God is compassion.

MEISTER ECKHART

Gd is a Gd of Lovingkindness.

ANNE ROIPHE

How excellent is thy lovingkindness, O God!

PSALMS 36:7

The essential thing to know about God is that God is Good. All the rest is secondary.

SIMONE WEIL

God is great, and therefore he will be sought: he is good, and therefore he will be found.

JOHN JAY

Love is the nature of God in action.

STELLA TERRILL MANN

Those without love have known nothing of God, for God is love.

I JOHN 4:8

I believe in God, who is for me spirit, love, the principle of all things. . . . I believe that the reason for life is for each of us simply to grow in love. I believe that this growth in love will contribute more than any other force to establish the Kingdom of God on earth.

LEO TOLSTOY

He rides pleasantly enough who is carried by the grace of God.

THOMAS À KEMPIS

Every friendship with God and every love between Him and a soul is the *only one* of its kind.

JANET ERSKINE STUART

He loves each of us, as if there were only one of us.

ST. AUGUSTINE

God is not indifferent to your need.
You have a thousand prayers,
but God has one.

ANNE SEXTON

It is not my business to think about myself. My business is to think about God. It is for God to think about me.

SIMONE WEIL

To believe in God's love
is to believe that He's passionately interested
in each of us personally
and continually.

LOUIS EVELY

The question "Are we significant to God?" is the religious question. It always was, and it always will be.

SEBASTIAN MOORE

We are all searching for the hug of God, our ultimate true love.

CAROLE STEWART MCDONNELL

The Infinite Goodness has such wide arms that it takes whatever turns to it.

DANTE ALIGHIERI

Our eagerness to throw ourselves into God's arms
is usually so well controlled
that we wouldn't get there very fast
unless He snatched us up Himself.

LOUIS EVELY

All desire the gifts of God,
but they do not desire God.

HANNAH MORE

Those who turn to God for comfort may find comfort but I do not think they will find God.

MIGNON McLAUGHLIN

They treated their God like a desk clerk with whom they lodged requests and complaints.

HELEN HUDSON

God is not a cosmic bell-boy for whom we can press a button to get things done.

HARRY EMERSON FOSDICK

The whole meaning of our existence and the one consuming desire of the heart of God is that we should let ourselves be loved.

RUTH BURROWS

God is that in which the heart of a man rests. If the resting is right the God is right. If the resting is wrong the God is wrong.

MARTIN LUTHER

With God all things are possible.

JESUS CHRIST

If God is your partner make your plans large.

MARTHA LUPTON

Be prepared at all times for the gifts of God and be ready always for new ones. For God is a thousand times more ready to give than we are.

MEISTER ECKHART

The well of Providence is deep. It is the buckets we bring to it that are small.

MARY WEBB

Today God gives milk
and I have the pail.

ANNE SEXTON

God's gifts put man's best dreams to shame.

ELIZABETH BARRETT BROWNING

All things work together for good to them that love God.

ROMANS 8:28

To accept the responsibility of being a child of God is to accept the best that life has to offer you.

STELLA TERRILL MANN

Having God one had all things.

RUTH BURROWS

Expect your every need to be met, expect the answer to every problem, expect abundance on every level, expect to grow spiritually.

EILEEN CADDY

Until I am essentially united with God, I can never have full rest or real happiness.

JULIAN OF NORWICH

I cannot walk an inch
without trying to walk to God.

ANNE SEXTON

How much did I hear of religion as a child? Very little, and yet my heart leaped when I heard the name of God. I do believe every soul has a tendency toward God.

DOROTHY DAY

We could not seek God unless He were seeking us.

THOMAS MERTON

Nowhere and never
And now and for ever
I look for a thing
That is looking for me.

SYDNEY CARTER

We cannot take a single step toward heaven. It is not in our power to travel in a vertical direction. If however we look heavenward for a long time, God comes and takes us up.

SIMONE WEIL

Heaven's net is indeed vast.
Though its meshes are wide, it misses nothing.

LAO-TZU

The lovers of God have no religion but God alone.

RUMI

God has no religion.

MOHANDAS K. GANDHI

Not I, but God in me.

DAG HAMMARSKJÖLD

God is my light and my salvation; whom shall I fear? God is the strength of my life; of whom shall I be afraid?

PSALMS 27:1

If God be for us, who can be against us?

ROMANS 8:31

We'll be religious insofar as we're amazed: "The Lord's performed wonders for me."

LOUIS EVELY

The starting point in the religious experience is wonder.

SEYMOUR COHEN

Awe precedes faith; it is at the root of faith. We must grow in awe in order to reach faith.

ABRAHAM JOSHUA HESCHEL

The highest point a man can attain is not Knowledge, or Virtue, or Goodness, or Victory, but something even greater, more heroic and more despairing: Sacred Awe!

NIKOS KAZANTZAKIS

Much of our understanding of God's action in our lives is achieved in hindsight. When a particular crisis or event in our life has passed we cry out in astonishment like Jacob, "The Lord is in this place and I never knew it."

SHEILA CASSIDY

If we are all made of God, it is our friends who remind us. We pass the gift of God to them. They pass it back to us when we need it most.

ERICA JONG

I could be whatever I wanted to be if I trusted that music, that song, that vibration of God that was *inside* of me.

SHIRLEY MACLAINE

When he sees little kids sitting in the backseat of cars, in those car seats that have steering wheels, with grim expressions of concentration on their faces, clearly convinced that their efforts are causing the car to do whatever it is doing, he thinks of himself and his relationship with God: God who drives along silently, gently amused, in the real driver's seat.

ANNE LAMOTT

Why indeed must "God" be a noun? Why not a verb—the most active and dynamic of all?

MARY DALY

He's not a "safe" or a "tame" God, securely lodged behind the bars of a distant heaven; he has the most annoying manner of showing up when we least want him; of confronting us in the strangest ways.

ROBERT MCAFEE BROWN

It is madness to wear ladies' . . . hats to church; we should all be wearing crash helmets. Ushers should issue life preservers and signal flares; they should lash us to our pews. For the sleeping God may wake someday and take offense, or the waking God may draw us out to where we can never return.

ANNIE DILLARD

Who can order the Holy? It is like a rain forest, dripping, lush, fecund, wild. We enter its abundance at our peril, for here we are called to the wholeness for which we long, but which requires all we are and can hope to be.

MARILYN SEWELL

The perpetual danger which besets religion is that it may substitute gentility and aestheticism for prophetic insight and power.

GEORGIA HARKNESS

A priest friend of mine has cautioned me away from the standard God of our childhoods, who loves and guides you and then, if you are bad, roasts you: God as high school principal in a gray suit who never remembered your name but is always leafing unhappily through your files.

ANNE LAMOTT

Ain't no way to read the bible and not think God white, she say. Then she sigh. When I found out I thought God was white, and a man, I lost interest.

ALICE WALKER

I saw God last night. Really? What's he like? Well, *he's* a *woman* and she's *Black*!

ANONYMOUS WOMAN

I met God. "What," he said, "you already?" "What," I said, "you still?"

LAURA RIDING JACKSON

THE SOUL

The life whereby we are joined into the body is called the soul.

ST. AUGUSTINE

It is not that we *have* a soul, we *are* a soul.

AMELIA E. BARR

A Soul is partly given, partly wrought.

ERICA JONG

The authentic self is the Soul made visible.

SARAH BAN BREATHNACH

The soul is partly in eternity and partly in time.

MARSILIO FICINO

The human soul develops up to the time of death.

HIPPOCRATES

The soul, like the moon,
is new, and always new again.

LALLESWARI

The soul can split the sky in two,
And let the face of God shine through.

EDNA ST. VINCENT MILLAY

Just as the soul is the life of the body, so God is the life of the soul.

St. Augustine

The human soul is a silent harp in God's quire, whose strings need only to be swept by the divine breath to chime in with the harmonies of creation.

Henry David Thoreau

Nothing in all nature is so lovely and so vigorous, so perfectly at home in its environment, as a fish in the sea. Its surroundings give to it a beauty, quality, and power which is not its own. We take it out, and at once a poor, limp dull thing, fit for nothing, is gasping away its life. So the soul, sunk in God, living the life of prayer, is supported, filled, transformed in beauty, by a vitality and a power which are not its own.

Evelyn Underhill

I began to think of the soul as if it were a castle
made of a single diamond or of very clear crystal, in
which there are many rooms, just as in Heaven
there are many mansions.

ST. TERESA OF AVILA

You could not discover the frontiers of the soul,
even if you traveled every road to do so; such is the
depth of its meaning.

HERACLITUS

The soul itself, the soul of each one of us, is to each
one of us a mystery. It hides in the dark and broods,
and consciousness cannot tell us of its workings.

OSCAR WILDE

The powers of the Soul are commensurate with its needs.

RALPH WALDO EMERSON

We are very strange creatures, so strange that, in my opinion at least, not a philosopher of them all has written the first sentence in the book of the soul.

W. MACNEILE DIXON

The Soul should always stand ajar.

EMILY DICKINSON

From the moment a soul has the grace to know God, she must seek.

MOTHER TERESA

Like the fish, swimming in the vast sea and resting in its deeps, and like the bird, boldly mounting high in the sky, so the soul feels its spirit freely moving through the vastness and the depth and the unutterable richnesses of love.

BEATRICE OF NAZARETH

An old mystic says somewhere, "God is an unutterable sigh in the innermost depths of the soul." With still greater justice, we may reverse the proposition, and say the soul is a never ending sigh after God.

THEODORE CHRISTLIEB

Feeling is the language of the soul.

NEALE DONALD WALSCH

Wilt thou one day, my soul, be good, simple, single, naked, plainer to see than the body surrounding thee?

MARCUS AURELIUS

No human soul is like any other human soul, and therefore the love of God for any human soul is infinite, for no other soul can satisfy the same need in God.

WILLIAM BUTLER YEATS

MMORTALITY

This world is not conclusion.
A sequel stands beyond —
Invisible, as music —
But positive, as sound.

EMILY DICKINSON

Eternity is not something that begins after you are dead. It is going on all the time. We are in it now.

CHARLOTTE PERKINS GILMAN

Everything science has taught me—and continues to teach me—strengthens my belief in the continuity of our spiritual existence after death. Nothing disappears without a trace.

WERNHER VON BRAUN

Neither experience nor science has given man the idea of immortality . . . . The idea of immortality rises from the very depths of his soul—he feels, he sees, he knows that he is immortal.

FRANÇOIS GUIZOT

Every natural longing has its natural satisfaction. If we thirst, God has created liquids to gratify thirst. If we are susceptible of attachment, there are beings to gratify our love. If we thirst for life and love eternal, it is likely that there are an eternal life and an eternal love to satisfy that craving.

FREDERICK WILLIAM ROBERTSON

Nothing short of an eternity could enable men to imagine, think, and feel, and to express all they have imagined, thought, and felt. Immortality, which is the spiritual desire, is the intellectual necessity.

EDWARD G. BULWER-LYTTON

We feel and know that we are eternal.

BARUCH SPINOZA

My belief in immortality, so far as I can divine its origin, and that is not far, seems to be connected with the same impulse which urges me to know myself. I can never know myself, but the closer I come to knowledge of myself the more certain I must feel that I am immortal, and, conversely, the more certain I am of my immortality the more intimately I must come to know myself.

EDWIN MUIR

Our Creator would never have made such lovely days, and have given us the deep hearts to enjoy them, unless we were meant to be immortal.

NATHANIEL HAWTHORNE

The blazing evidence of immortality is our dissatisfaction with any other solution.

RALPH WALDO EMERSON

If I find in myself a desire which no experience in this world can satisfy, the most probable explanation is that I was made for another world.

C.S. LEWIS

Not all the subtleties of metaphysics can make me doubt a moment of the immortality of the soul, and of a beneficent providence. I feel it, I believe it, I desire it, I hope it, and will defend it to my last breath.

JEAN JACQUES ROUSSEAU

I believe in the immortality of the soul because I have within me immortal longings.

HELEN KELLER

I have
Immortal longings in me.

WILLIAM SHAKESPEARE

Biggest affirmative argument I know in favor of "If a man die, shall he live again?" is just the way you feel inside you that nothin' can stop you from livin' on.

BESS STREETER ALDRICH

I want to go on living even after my death!

ANNE FRANK

We do not believe in immortality because we can prove it, but we try to prove it because we cannot help believing it.

HARRIET MARTINEAU

All men desire to be immortal.

THEODORE PARKER

We exclaim . . . "How time flies!" as though the universal form of our experience were again and again a novelty. It is as strange as if a fish were repeatedly surprised at the wetness of water. And that would be strange indeed; unless of course the fish were destined to become, one day, a land animal.

C.S. LEWIS

There is adventure in eternal life. There is none in eternal death. I am all for adventure.

JOHN WILLIAM DUNNE

Christ ... even restored the severed ear of the soldier who came to arrest Him—a fact that allows us to hope the resurrection will reflect a considerable attention to detail.

MARILYNNE ROBINSON

Sometimes I think the resurrection of the body, unless much improved in construction, a mistake!

EVELYN UNDERHILL

What's so good about a heaven where, one of these days, you're going to get your embarrassing old body back?

MARSHA NORMAN

It is rather depressing to think that one will still be oneself when one is dead, but I dare say one won't be so critical then.

ANGELA THIRKELL

Millions long for immortality who don't know what to do with themselves on a rainy Sunday afternoon.

SUSAN ERTZ

HE SACREDNESS OF DAILY LIFE

Your daily life is your temple and your religion. Whenever you enter into it take with you your all.

KAHLIL GIBRAN

Every day is a god, each day is a god, and holiness holds forth in time.

ANNIE DILLARD

To the poet, to the philosopher, to the saint, all things are friendly and sacred, all events profitable, all days holy, all men divine.

RALPH WALDO EMERSON

True spirituality does not exist without love of life.

NATHANIEL BRANDEN

To the soul, the ordinary is sacred and the everyday is the primary source of religion.

THOMAS MOORE

The whole inhabited earth is sacred space in which God lives, breathes, and acts.

CARTER HEYWARD

To survive we must begin to know sacredness. The pace which most of us live prevents this.

CHRYSTOS

We are naturally reverent beings, but much of our natural reverence has been torn away from us because we have been born into a world that hurries. There is no time to be reverent with the earth or with each other. We are all hurrying into progress. And for all our hurrying we lose sight of our true nature a little more each day.

MACRINA WIEDERKEHR

If we haven't found God on earth,
we won't find Him in heaven.

LOUIS EVELY

One of the hardest lessons we have to learn in this
life, and one that many persons never learn, is to see
the divine, the celestial, the pure in the common,
the near at hand—to see that heaven lies about us
here in this world.

JOHN BURROUGHS

Heaven is a near
translatable thing;
it's here,
it's there.

H.D.

My soul can find no staircase to Heaven unless it be through Earth's loveliness.

MICHELANGELO

Human experience is already experience of God. Our journey on earth is already a journey to heaven. Seeing a sunrise or a flower is already seeing God.

CARLO CARRETTO

Faith strips the mask from the world and reveals God in everything. It makes nothing impossible and renders meaningless such words as anxiety, danger, and fear, so that the believer goes through life calmly and peacefully, with profound joy—like a child, hand in hand with his mother.

CHARLES DE FOUCAULD

Anxiety is the rust of life, destroying its brightness and weakening its power. A childlike and abiding trust in Providence is its best preventive and remedy.

TRYON EDWARDS

Listen, God love everything you love—and a mess of stuff you don't. But more than anything else, God love admiration . . . . I think it pisses God off if you walk by the color purple in a field somewhere and don't notice it.

ALICE WALKER

God changes his appearance every second. Blessed is the man who can recognize him in all his disguises. One moment he is a glass of fresh water, the next your son bouncing on your knees or an enchanting woman, or perhaps merely a morning walk.

NIKOS KAZANTZAKIS

People usually consider walking on water or in thin air a miracle. But I think the real miracle is not to walk either on water or in thin air, but to walk on earth. Every day we are engaged in a miracle which we don't even recognize: a blue sky, white clouds, green leaves, the black, curious eyes of a child—our own two eyes. All is a miracle.

THICH NHAT HANH

Since human life is sacred, what we have traditionally labeled "secular" is sacred.

MALCOLM BOYD

The veil between us and the divine is more permeable than we imagine.

SUE PATTON THOELE

The flesh is as spiritual as the soul, and the soul is as natural as the flesh.

JANE ROBERTS

Mind is matter, matter is mind. Matter does not exist outside of mind. Mind does not exist outside of matter. Each is in the other.

NAGARJUNA

Those who see any difference between soul and body have neither.

OSCAR WILDE

This kind of split makes me crazy, this territorializing of the holy. Here God may dwell. Here God may not dwell. It contradicts everything in my experience, which says: God dwells where I dwell. Period.

NANCY MAIRS

The divorce of our so-called spiritual life from our daily activities is a fatal dualism.

M.P. FOLLETT

Life, to be happy at all, must be in its way a sacrament, and it is a failure in religion to divorce it from the holy acts of everyday, of ordinary human existence.

FREYA STARK

As we begin to sense the divine in the "ordinary," our "ordinary" lives will become quite extraordinary.

RICHARD CARLSON

There is nothing so secular that it cannot be sacred.

MADELEINE L'ENGLE

Spiritual love is a position of standing with one hand extended into the universe and one hand extended into the world, letting ourselves be a conduit for passing energy.

CHRISTINA BALDWIN

God is in the sadness and the laughter, in the bitter and the sweet. There is a divine purpose behind everything—and therefore a divine presence *in* everything.

NEALE DONALD WALSCH

All emotions, all human activities, and all spheres of life have deep roots in the mysteries of the soul, and therefore are holy.

THOMAS MOORE

To receive the love of God is to recognize it is all around us, above us, and beneath us; speaking to us through every person, every flower, every trial and situation. Stop knocking on the door: You're already inside!

RICHARD ROHR

Spirituality promotes passivity when the domain of spirit is defined as outside the world. When this world is the terrain of spirit, we ourselves become actors in the story, and this world becomes the realm in which the sacred must be honored and freedom created.

STARHAWK

To the analytical mind, the universe is broken apart. It is split into the known and unknown, into the seen and unseen. But, in the mystic contemplation, all things are seen as one. The mystic mind tends to hold the world together.

ABRAHAM JOSHUA HESCHEL

Holy persons draw to themselves all that is earthly.

HILDEGARD OF BINGEN

Living the spiritual life means living life as one unified reality. The forces of darkness are the forces that split, divide and set in opposition. The forces of light unite. Literally, the word "diabolic" means dividing. The demon divides; the Spirit unites.

HENRI J.M. NOUWEN

There is no enlightenment outside daily life.

THICH NHAT NANH

The life of the spirit, by integrating us in the real order established by God, puts us in the fullest possible contact with reality—not as we imagine it, but as it really is.

THOMAS MERTON

Spirituality is the sacred center out of which all life comes, including Mondays and Tuesdays and rainy Saturday afternoons in all their mundane and glorious detail . . . . The spiritual journey is the soul's life commingling with ordinary life.

CHRISTINA BALDWIN

Awareness of the sacred in life is what holds our world together, and the lack of awareness of the sacred is what is tearing it apart.

JOAN CHITTISTER

Religious man lives in an open world and . . . his existence is open to the world. This means that religious man is accessible to an infinite series of experiences that could be termed cosmic. Such experiences are always religious, for the world is sacred.

MIRCEA ELIADE

Let there be no disappointment when obedience keeps you busy in outward tasks. If it sends you to the kitchen, remember that the Lord walks among the pots and pans.

ST. TERESA OF AVILA

When a man, a woman, see their little daily tasks as integral portions of the one great work, they are no longer drudges but co-workers with God.

ANNIE BESANT

Works do not sanctify us—but we are to sanctify our works.

MEISTER ECKHART

The tension between the call to the desert and to the market place arises not from the greater presence of God in one or the other but from our varying psychological needs to apprehend him in different ways.

SHEILA CASSIDY

To the true servant of God every place is the right place and every time is the right time.

ST. CATHERINE OF SIENA

One should hallow all that one does in one's natural life. One eats in holiness, tastes the taste of food in holiness, and the table becomes an altar. One works in holiness, and he raises up the sparks which hide themselves in all tools. One walks in holiness across the fields, and the soft songs of all herbs, which they voice to God, enter into the song of our soul.

MARTIN BUBER

All things are woven together and the common bond is sacred, and scarcely one thing is foreign to another, for they have been arranged together in their places and together make the same ordered Universe.

MARCUS AURELIUS

One of the most important—and most neglected elements in the beginnings of the interior life is the ability to respond to reality, to see the value and the beauty in ordinary things, to come alive to the splendor that is all around us in the creatures of God.

THOMAS MERTON

We cannot talk with God if we abandon the world to itself. We can only talk with God when we put our arms, as well as we can, around the world, that is when we carry God's truth and justice to all.

MARTIN BUBER

BECOMING HUMAN

We are not human beings learning to be spiritual;
we are spiritual beings learning to be human.

JACQUELYN SMALL

We're not human beings that have occasional spiritual experiences—it's the other way around: we're
spiritual beings that have occasional human experiences.

DEEPAK CHOPRA

We're souls having a human experience.

BRIAN WEISS

The spiritual path ... is simply the journey of living our lives. Everyone is on a spiritual path; most people just don't know it.

MARIANNE WILLIAMSON

One of the most important things that any religion can teach us is what it means to be human.

HAROLD S. KUSHNER

Each of us has some kind of vocation. . . . For each one of us, there is only one thing necessary: to fulfill our own destiny, according to God's will, to be what God wants us to be.

THOMAS MERTON

Spiritual life is a matter of becoming who you *truly* are. It's not becoming Catherine of Siena, or some other saint, but who *you* are. It sounds easy enough, but being who you truly are is work, courage and faith.

RICHARD ROHR

The Glory of God is a human being who is fully alive!

ST. IRENAEUS

An authentic life is the most personal form of worship. Everyday life has become my prayer.

SARAH BAN BREATHNACH

What you are is God's gift to you; what you make of it is your gift to God.

ANTHONY DALLA VILLA

We can search for and attain to only one being, that one which was given us, which is within us and which awaits its birth from ourselves. Each day I feel that I leave myself a little more, the better to go toward my encounter with myself.

GEORGETTE LEBLANC

My business is not to remake myself,
But make the absolute best of what God made.

ROBERT BROWNING

Maybe the tragedy of the human race was that we had forgotten we were each Divine.

SHIRLEY MACLAINE

There is no good in trying to be more spiritual than God. God never means man to be a purely spiritual creature . . . . He likes matter. He created it.

C.S. LEWIS

LOVE ONE ANOTHER

A new commandment I give to you, that you love one another.

JOHN 13:34

We are learning from the teaching and example of Jesus that life itself is a religion, that nothing is more sacred than a human being, that the end of all right institutions, whether the home or the church or an educational establishment, or a government, is the development of the human soul.

ANNA HOWARD SHAW

Love . . . puts you in a right relation with God and others, reciprocal rather than hierarchical. . . . But the great commandment is extralegal. Love cannot be forced. It must be chosen. You love not out of dread but out of your own fullness. It's what you were made for. When you fail at it, you aren't sent to prison, or to the electric chair, or to hell. You are commanded again: Love.

NANCY MAIRS

We cannot be sure if we are loving God, although we may have good reasons for believing that we are, but we can know quite well if we are loving our neighbor. And be certain that, the farther advanced you find you are in this, the greater the love you will have for God.

ST. TERESA OF AVILA

The love of our neighbor in all its fullness simply means being able to say to him, "What are you going through?"

SIMONE WEIL

Spiritual energy brings compassion into the real world. With compassion, we see benevolently our own human condition and the condition of our fellow beings. We drop prejudice. We withhold judgment.

CHRISTINA BALDWIN

I sought to hear the
voice of God
And climbed the
topmost steeple,
But God declared:
"Go down again —
I dwell among
the people."

JOHN HENRY NEWMAN

In the faces of men and women I see God.

WALT WHITMAN

When you see God in everyone, everyone will see
God in you.

ANONYMOUS

Remember that you are all people and that all people are you.

Joy Harjo

Few are the giants of the soul who actually feel that the human race is their family circle.

Elizabeth Wray Taylor

Each being is sacred—meaning that each has inherent value that cannot be ranked in a hierarchy or compared to the value of another being.

Starhawk

God is present in the confusion and dislocation of the world. One encounters God not by turning one's back on that world but by plunging into it with the faith that the divine-human encounter occurs in the midst of the encounter of human with human, especially in the struggle to create signs of the coming of God's reign of peace and justice.

HARVEY COX

All theology knowingly or not is by definition always engaged for or against the oppressed.

ELISABETH SCHÜSSLER FIORENZA

The feeding of those that are hungry is a form of contemplation.

SIMONE WEIL

When half the world is still plagued by terror and distress, you stop guiltily sometimes in the midst of your house-laughter and wonder if you've a right to it. Ought *any* of us to laugh, until *all* of us can again, you ask yourself, sometimes.

MARGARET LEE RUNBECK

If you're going to care about the fall of the sparrow you can't pick and choose who's going to be the sparrow. It's everybody.

MADELEINE L'ENGLE

Love needs to be proved by action.

ST. THÉRÈSE OF LISIEUX

I am often praying for others when I should be doing things for them. It's so much easier to pray for a bore than to go and see him.

C.S. LEWIS

If prayers are going to be answered at all, human beings probably have to answer them for each other.

MARGARET LEE RUNBECK

My brother doesn't want a keeper. He wants a brother.

MALCOLM BOYD

The fault of others is easily perceived, but that of one's self is difficult to perceive; a man winnows his neighbor's faults like chaff, but his own fault he hides, as a cheat hides an unlucky cast of the die.

BUDDHA

Spiritual maturity begins when we realize that we are God's guests in this world. We are not house-holders, but pilgrims; not landlords, but tenants; not owners, but guests.

C. WILLARD FETTER

Neither saints nor angels have ever increased my faith in this enigma Life; but what are called "common men and women" have increased it.

PHYLLIS BOTTOME

He that loveth not, knoweth not God; for God is love.

I JOHN 4:8

God is love. And in every moment of genuine love we are dwelling in God and God in us.

PAUL TILLICH

The blessings that we give to each other are expressions of the blessing that rests on us from all eternity.

HENRI J.M. NOUWEN

Stretch out your hand!—let no human soul wait for a benediction.

MARIE CORELLI

Religion seeks a love beyond any love that has ever developed between human associates. It seeks a love which, so far as human association is concerned, is only a possibility. But precisely because religion does afford a vision of the possibility, it stimulates love-making between parent and child and David and Jonathan and man and woman to the end of achieving more love between humans. And love-making is one of the great arts of living.

HENRY NELSON WIEMAN

 PRAYER

Prayer is conversation with God.

ST. CLEMENT OF ALEXANDRIA

Prayer is a long rope with a strong hold.

HARRIET BEECHER STOWE

To pray is to expose ourselves to God as we do to heat or sunlight.

LOUIS EVELY

Prayer is the language of the heart.

GRACE AGUILAR

Prayer is the natural language of love.

JOAN BROWN CAMPBELL

Prayer, like radium, is a luminous and self-generating form of energy.

ALEXIS CARREL

Prayer is the mortar that holds our house together.

MOTHER TERESA

Prayer begins where human capacity ends.

MARIAN ANDERSON

Prayer begins where expression ends . . . . Words
can only open the door, and we can only weep on
the threshold of our incommunicable thirst after the
incomprehensible.

ABRAHAM JOSHUA HESCHEL

We don't have all the answers. Perhaps prayer is simply a time we set aside to acknowledge that reality.

MARY E. HUNT

Prayer is an exercise of the spirit, as thought is of the mind.

MARY F. SMITH

Prayer oneth the soul to God.

JULIAN OF NORWICH

The purpose of prayer is not the same as the purpose of speech. The purpose of speech is to inform; the purpose of prayer is to partake.

ABRAHAM JOSHUA HESCHEL

Prayer is naught else but a yearning of soul. . . . It draws down the great God into the little heart; it drives the hungry soul up to the plenitude of God; it brings together these two lovers, God and the soul, in a wondrous place where they speak much of love.

MECHTHILD OF MAGDEBURG

O my Lord, the stars are shining and the eyes of men are closed, and kings have shut their doors and every lover is alone with his beloved, and here am I alone with Thee.

RABI'A THE MYSTIC

Prayer is not asking for things—not even for the best things; it is going where they are.

GERALD HEARD

Prayer is not for the sake of something else. *We pray in order to pray.*

ABRAHAM JOSHUA HESCHEL

Prayer is the sum of our relationship with God. We are what we pray. The degree of our faith is the degree of our prayer. Our ability to love is our ability to pray.

CARLO CARRETTO

Prayer is a principal means for opening oneself to the power and love of God that is already *there*— in the depths of reality.

JAMES A. PIKE

Prayer is the opening of the soul to God so that he can speak to us.

GEORGIA HARKNESS

Prayer has the power to generate insight; it often endows us with an understanding not attainable by speculation. Some of our deepest insights, decisions and attitudes are born in moments of prayer.

ABRAHAM JOSHUA HESCHEL

The only certainties that don't break down are those acquired in prayer.

REINHOLD SCHNEIDER

Prayer does not change God, but it changes him who prays.

SÖREN KIERKEGAARD

We kneel, how weak! we rise, how full of power!

R.C. TRENCH

Our prayers must spring from the indigenous soil of our own personal confrontation with the Spirit of God in our lives. . . . Prayer must be personal, embedded in the ground of one's own being as a person meeting God.

MALCOLM BOYD

I believe that true prayer makes us into what we imagine. To pray to God leads to becoming like God.

HENRI J.M. NOUWEN

Prayer is essentially a process by which ideals are enabled to become operative in our lives. It may be more than this, but it is at least this.

GEORGIA HARKNESS

No man has ever prayed without learning something.

RALPH WALDO EMERSON

No sincere prayer leaves us where it finds us.

STELLA TERRILL MANN

It could not happen that any man or woman could pray for a single moment without some good result.

ALEXIS CARREL

I never went to bed in my life and I never ate a meal in my life without saying a prayer. I know my prayers have been answered thousands of times, and I know that I never said a prayer in my life without something good coming of it.

JACK DEMPSEY

Prayer is an attempt to count the stars of our souls.

JAMES MELVIN WASHINGTON

The sense of the holy manifests itself chiefly by prayer.

ALEXIS CARREL

Prayer is *our* humble *answer* to the inconceivable surprise of living. It is all we can offer in return for the mystery by which we live.

ABRAHAM JOSHUA HESCHEL

Prayer is the way to both the heart of God and the heart of the world.

HENRI J.M. NOUWEN

Every time you pray, if your prayer is sincere, there will be new feeling and new meaning in it, which will give you fresh courage, and you will understand that prayer is an education.

FEODOR DOSTOEVSKI

As for prayer . . . follow your own way of speaking to God sincerely, lovingly, confidently and simply, as your heart dictates.

JANE DE CHANTAL

When thou prayest, rather let thy heart be without words than thy words be without heart.

JOHN BUNYAN

Complaint is the largest tribute Heaven receives, and the sincerest part of our devotion.

JONATHAN SWIFT

Every prayer reduces itself to this: "Great God, grant that twice two be not four."

IVAN TURGENEV

The best prayers have often more groans than words.

JOHN BUNYAN

If a care is too small to be turned into a prayer, it is too small to be made into a burden.

CORRIE TEN BOOM

The most simple rule for good prayer is honesty and humility. One can never go wrong with those two. Talk honestly to God. Don't give God the self you think you're supposed to be. Give God yourself in your nakedness, who you really are, even if that means giving God your anger or distractions.

RICHARD ROHR

Although I try
to hold the single thought
of Buddha's teaching in my heart,
I cannot help but hear
the many crickets' voices calling as well.

Izumi Shikibu

He prayed as he breathed, forming no words and
making no specific requests, only holding in his
heart, like broken birds in cupped hands, all those
people who were in stress or grief.

Ellis Peters

Prayer is the soul's sincere desire, uttered or unex-
pressed.

James Montgomery

He didn't know exactly what he wanted to pray for; in which he was like most other people. For our real prayer, if we had the wits or the courage to formulate it, would be a general plea for everything to be all right for ever.

ANGELA THIRKELL

For me, prayer means launching out of the heart towards God; it means lifting up one's eyes, quite simply, to heaven, a cry of grateful love, from the crest of joy or the trough of despair; it's a vast, supernatural force which opens out my heart, and binds me close to Jesus.

ST. THÉRÈSE OF LISIEUX

We all know how to pray better than we practice what we know!

GEORGIA HARKNESS

Prayer is a psychological place, a spiritual place, a place where we go to get out of ourselves, a place created and inhabited by God.

RICHARD ROHR

Prayer is not a stratagem for occasional use, a refuge to resort to now and then. It is rather like an established residence for the innermost self. All things have a home: the bird has a nest, the fox has a hole, the bee has a hive. A soul without prayer is a soul without a home.

ABRAHAM JOSHUA HESCHEL

Prayer, to the thinking person, is almost inescapable.

MARJORIE HOLMES

Prayer enlarges the heart until it is capable of containing God's gift of himself.

MOTHER TERESA

Prayer is not hearing yourself talk, but being silent, staying silent and waiting until you hear God.

SÖREN KIERKEGAARD

Consistent prayer is the desire to do right.

MARY BAKER EDDY

The wish to pray is prayer in itself.

GEORGES BERNANOS

Pray inwardly, even if you do not enjoy it. It does good, though you feel nothing. Yes, even though you think you are doing nothing.

JULIAN OF NORWICH

Prayer itself is God. It's not an activity to get God to like me, or to talk to God. It's not something that I do for God; prayer is God in me loving God outside of me, and God outside of me loving God in me.

RICHARD ROHR

God is the one who prays and loves in us.

LOUIS EVELY

Words, created *by* and used *in* our conscious life, are not the essence of prayer. The essence of prayer is the act of God who is working in us and raises our whole being to Himself. . . . Only in terms of wordless sighs can we approach God, and even these sighs are His work in us.

PAUL TILLICH

Prayer, crystallized in words, assigns a permanent wave length on which the dialogue has to be continued, even when our mind is occupied with other matters.

DAG HAMMARSKJÖLD

Praying means placing ourselves at God's disposal so that, for a moment or two, he may accomplish what he has always wanted to do in us and what we never give him a chance to.

LOUIS EVELY

Prayer is a law of the universe, like gravity. You don't even have to believe in God to ask.

SOPHY BURNHAM

A prayer in its simplest definition is merely a wish turned Godward.

PHILLIPS BROOKS

To pray it is only necessary to make the effort of reaching out toward God.

ALEXIS CARREL

Certain thoughts are prayers. There are moments when, whatever be the attitude of the body, the soul is on its knees.

VICTOR HUGO

The life of prayer is so great and various there is something in it for everyone. It is like a garden which grows everything, from alpines to potatoes.

EVELYN UNDERHILL

You can do more than praying after you have prayed. You can never do more than praying before you have prayed.

CORRIE TEN BOOM

More things are wrought by prayer
Than this world dreams of.

ALFRED, LORD TENNYSON

Let everyone try and find that as a result of daily prayer he adds something new to his life.

MOHANDAS K. GANDHI

It's not that we pray and God answers; our praying is already God answering.

RICHARD ROHR

I believe that God prays in us and through us, whether we are praying or not (and whether we believe in God or not). So, any prayer on my part is a conscious response to what God is already doing in my life.

MALCOLM BOYD

A spirituality without a prayer life is no spirituality at all, and it will not last beyond the first defeat. Prayer is an opening of the self so that the Word of God can break in and make us new. Prayer unmasks. Prayer converts. Prayer impels. Prayer sustains us on the way.

JOAN CHITTISTER

Holiness is not something that follows from prayer; we pray because we are holy.

JOHN CATOIR

This conversion into prayer of our everyday joys, sorrows, hopes and desires is at first a conscious labor, but after a while it becomes second nature, so that converse with God becomes inextricably and wonderfully woven into the fabric of our lives.

SHEILA CASSIDY

Prayer should be the key of the day and the lock of the night.

THOMAS FULLER

Seven days without prayer makes one weak.

ANONYMOUS

If you are too busy to pray, you are too busy.

ANONYMOUS

What ascends up in prayer descends to us again in blessings. It is like the rain which just now fell, and which had been drawn up from the ground in vapors to the clouds before it descended from them to the earth in that refreshing shower.

HANNAH MORE

With prayer, one can go on cheerfully and even happily. Without prayer, how grim a journey!

DOROTHY DAY

You can't defeat a praying man. He finds his answers everywhere he looks.

MARGARET LEE RUNBECK

I strain toward God; God strains toward me. I ache for God; God aches for me. Prayer is mutual yearning, mutual straining, mutual aching.

MACRINA WIEDERKEHR

The dialogue between God and humanity is the give-and-take of self-revelation and response. . . . In prayer God is gradually disclosing himself, revealing herself.

RICHARD ROHR

More than 130 controlled laboratory studies show, in general, that prayer or a prayerlike state of compassion, empathy, and love can bring about healthful changes in many types of living things, from humans to bacteria. This does not mean that prayer *always* works, any more than drugs and surgery always work but that, statistically speaking, prayer is effective.

LARRY DOSSEY

Make every effort to pray from the heart. Even if you do not succeed, in the eyes of the Lord the effort is precious.

THE GATES OF PRAYER:
THE NEW UNION JEWISH PRAYER BOOK

We have to pray long, but with few words.

LOUIS EVELY

Being useless and silent in the presence of our God belongs to the core of all prayer.

HENRI J.M. NOUWEN

In vocal prayer we speak to God; in mental prayer he speaks to us. It is then that God pours Himself into us.

MOTHER TERESA

In mental prayer, shut your eyes, shut your mouth, and open your heart.

ST. JOHN-MARIE-BAPTISTE VIANNEY

The only way to pray is to pray; and the way to pray well is to pray much.

JOHN CHAPMAN

I pray by breathing.

THOMAS MERTON

Meditate in the morning and evening and at night before you go to bed. Sit quietly for about two minutes. You will find everything in your life falling into place and your prayers answered.

YOGASWAMI

In the silence of the heart God speaks. If you face God in prayer and silence, God will speak to you. Then you will know that you are nothing. It is only when you realize your nothingness, your emptiness, that God can fill you with Himself. Souls of prayer are souls of great silence.

MOTHER TERESA

In saying my prayers, I discovered the voice of an innermost self, the raw nerve of my identity.

GELSEY KIRKLAND

Prayer gives a man the opportunity of getting to know a gentleman he hardly ever meets. I do not mean his maker, but himself.

WILLIAM R. INGE

I believe the old cliché, "God helps those who help themselves," is not only misleading but often dead wrong. My most spectacular answers to prayers have come when I was so helpless, so out of control as to be able to do nothing at all for myself.

CATHERINE MARSHALL

We seem to be much more comfortable talking about our sex lives than we are sharing information with each other about how we pray. Perhaps this is because praying may be the most personal and intimate thing we do.

SHERRY RUTH ANDERSON AND PATRICIA HOPKINS

Prayer gives you no immediate payoff. You get no immediate feedback or sense of success. True prayer, in that sense, probably is the most courageous and countercultural thing an American will ever do.

RICHARD ROHR

Prayer is not our most natural response to the world. Left to our own impulses, we will always want to do something else before we pray.

HENRI J.M. NOUWEN

You pray in your distress and in your need; would that you might pray also in the fullness of your joy and in your days of abundance.

KAHLIL GIBRAN

To pray only when in peril is to use safety belts only in heavy traffic.

CORRIE TEN BOOM

God is greater than my mind and my heart, and what is really happening in the house of prayer is not measurable in terms of human success and failure.

HENRI J.M. NOUWEN

Prayer can be an easy substitute for real spirituality. It would be impossible to have spirituality without prayer, of course, but it is certainly possible to pray without having a spirituality at all. How do you know? "Am I becoming kinder?" is a good place to start.

JOAN CHITTISTER

Some folks regard prayer as an umbrella to use only when it's raining—and have the same trouble finding it when they need it.

ANONYMOUS

Is prayer your steering wheel or your spare tire?

CORRIE TEN BOOM

AMILIAR PRAYERS

Now I lay me down to sleep,
I pray the Lord, my soul to keep;
If I should die before I wake,
I pray the Lord, my soul to take.

THE NEW ENGLAND PRIMER

God, give us the serenity to accept what cannot be
changed; Give us the courage to change what
should be changed; Give us the wisdom to distin-
guish one from the other.

REINHOLD NIEBUHR

Lord, make me an instrument of Thy peace; where
there is hatred, let me sow love; where there is
injury, pardon; where there is doubt, faith; where
there is despair, hope; where there is darkness, light;
and where there is sadness, joy.

ST. FRANCIS OF ASSISI

Lead, kindly Light, amid the encircling gloom,
Lead Thou me on!

JOHN HENRY NEWMAN

Go placidly amid the noise and haste, and remember what peace there may be in silence. As far as possible without surrender be on good terms with all persons. . . . Most important of all, be at peace with God. Remember, prayer will always lead to peace. Be happy! With all its sham, drudgery, and broken dreams, it is still a beautiful world!

ANONYMOUS, "DESIDERATA"

God be in my head and in my understanding;
God be in my eyes and in my looking;
God be in my mouth and in my speaking;
God be in my heart and in my thinking;
God be at mine end and at my departing.

EASTERN PRAYER

My Lord God, I have no idea where I am going. I do not see the road ahead of me. I cannot know for certain where it will end. Nor do I really know myself, and the fact that I think that I am following your will does not mean that I am actually doing so. But I believe that the desire to please you does in fact please you. And I hope I have that desire in all that I am doing. I hope that I will never do anything apart from that desire. And I know that if I do this you will lead me by the right road though I may know nothing about it. Therefore, will I trust you always though I may seem to be lost and in the shadow of death. I will not fear, you are ever with me, and you will never leave me to face my perils alone.

THOMAS MERTON

Come, O Creator, Spirit blest!
And in our souls take up Thy rest;
Come, with Thy grace and heavenly aid,
To fill the hearts which Thou has made.

MARY ARTEMISIA LATHBURY

O Lord! thou knowest how busy I must be this day:
if I forget thee, do not thou forget me.

JACOB ASTLEY

All shall be well
and all shall be well
and all manner of thing shall be well.

JULIAN OF NORWICH

GRATITUDE

If the only prayer you say in your entire life is
"Thank You," that would suffice.

MEISTER ECKHART

For all that has been—Thanks! To all that shall
be—Yes!

DAG HAMMARSKJÖLD

One single, thankful thought directed to heaven is
the most perfect prayer.

GOTTHOLD EPHRAIM LESSING

In acknowledgment lies depth. Thank you.
Thank you.
Just this.

DAVID K. REYNOLDS

Now let the soul number its gains and count its trea-
sures. They are so fine that they refine the hands
which count them.

PHILLIPS BROOKS

It is gratefulness which makes the soul great.

ABRAHAM JOSHUA HESCHEL

Say alleluia always, no matter the time of day, no matter the season of life.

BENEDICT OF NURSIA

Treasure the gift
Of spendthrift heaven.

JAMES KIRKUP

I would maintain that thanks are the highest form of thought; and that gratitude is happiness doubled by wonder.

G.K. CHESTERTON

To those leaning on the sustaining infinite, today is big with blessings.

MARY BAKER EDDY

Once you understand that God is the center of the universe, it's all very simple. Not a day goes by that I don't say, "Thank you. I'm truly blessed."

OPRAH WINFREY

Before me, even as behind,
God is, and all is well.

JOHN GREENLEAF WHITTIER

All the way to heaven is heaven.

ST. CATHERINE OF SIENA

AITH

Faith is the subtle chain which binds us to the infinite.

ELIZABETH OAKES SMITH

Faith is a gift of the spirit that allows the soul to remain attached to its own unfolding.

THOMAS MOORE

Faith is the soul riding at anchor.

JOSH BILLINGS

Faith is a belief in what you do not yet see, and the reward of faith is to see what you believe.

ST. AUGUSTINE

All I have seen teaches me to trust the Creator for all I have not seen.

RALPH WALDO EMERSON

Faith is the marriage of God and the Soul.

ST. JOHN OF THE CROSS

Faith is the centerpiece of a connected life. It allows us to live by the grace of invisible strands. It is a belief in a wisdom superior to our own. Faith becomes a teacher in the absence of fact.

TERRY TEMPEST WILLIAMS

Faith is not *being sure*. It is *not being sure*, but betting with your last cent.

MARY JEAN IRION

Faith is a process of leaping into the abyss not on the basis of any certainty about where we shall land, but rather on the belief that we *shall* land.

CARTER HEYWARD

If it can be verified, we don't need faith. . . . Faith is for that which lies on the *other* side of reason. Faith is what makes life bearable, with all its tragedies and ambiguities and sudden, startling joys.

MADELEINE L'ENGLE

Faith . . . is nothing at all tangible. It is simply believing God; and, like sight, it is nothing apart from its object. You might as well shut your eyes and look inside, and see whether you have sight, as to look inside to discover whether you have faith.

HANNAH WHITALL SMITH

Faith is an act of rational choice which determines us to act as if certain things were true and in the confident expectation that they will prove to be true.

WILLIAM R. INGE

A faith is that which is able to survive a mood.

G.K. CHESTERTON

Faith given back to us after a night of doubt is a stronger thing, and far more valuable to us than faith that has never been tested.

ELIZABETH GOUDGE

Faith isn't so much to believe that God *is* as to believe that God is *for you*.

RICHARD ROHR

It is the heart which experiences God, and not the reason. This, then, is faith: God felt by the heart, not by the reason.

BLAISE PASCAL

When a man sits in the warm sunshine, do you ask him for proof of it? He feels—that is all. And we feel—that is all. We want no proof of our God. We feel, we feel!

OLIVE SCHREINER

I do not seek to understand in order to believe but I believe in order to understand. For I believe even this: that I shall not understand unless I believe.

ST. ANSELM

The deepest levels of faith will still feel like confusion—but you are no longer confused by your confusion!

RICHARD ROHR

Faith indeed tells what the senses do not tell, but not the contrary of what they see. It is above them and not contrary to them.

BLAISE PASCAL

Faith is not belief. Belief is passive. Faith is active.

EDITH HAMILTON

Faith walks simply, childlike, between the darkness of human life and the hope of what is to come.

CATHERINE DE HUECK DOHERTY

To me, *faith* is not just a noun but also a verb.

JIMMY CARTER

Faith is that quality or power by which the things desired become the things possessed.

KATHRYN KUHLMAN

All things are possible to one who believes.

ST. BERNARD OF CLAIRVAUX

Without faith, nothing is possible. With it, nothing is impossible.

MARY MCLEOD BETHUNE

Faith is the substance of things hoped for, the evidence of things not seen.

HEBREWS 11:1

To one who waits, all things reveal themselves, so long as you have the courage not to deny in the darkness what you have seen in the light.

COVENTRY PATMORE

For him who has faith,
The last miracle
Shall be greater than the first.

DAG HAMMARSKJÖLD

Faith is so rare—and religion so common—because no one wants to live between first base and second base. Faith is the in-between space where you're not sure you'll make it to second base. You've let go of one thing and haven't yet latched onto another. Most of us choose the security of first base.

RICHARD ROHR

It's a condition of faith that it gets lost from time to time, or at least mislaid.

P.D. JAMES

Who has seen the wind?
Neither you nor I:
But when the trees bow down their heads
The wind is passing by.

CHRISTINA ROSSETTI

Faith strips the mask from the world and reveals God in everything. It makes nothing impossible and renders meaningless such words as anxiety, danger, and fear, so that the believer goes through life calmly and peacefully, with profound joy—like a child, hand in hand with his mother.

CHARLES DE FOUCAULD

Imagine walking into a darkened room. We put our hands in front of us, afraid we are going to bump into a piece of furniture or slip on a rug. We walk very slowly. This is very much what God calls us to on the journey of faith.

RICHARD ROHR

Doubt is not the opposite of faith; it is one element of faith.

PAUL TILLICH

Faith and doubt both are needed—not as antagonists but working side by side—to take us around the unknown curve.

LILLIAN SMITH

Faith is always an adventure.

ELSIE CHAMBERLAIN

The believer who has never doubted will hardly convert a doubter.

MARIE VON EBNER-ESCHENBACH

OLINESS

Holiness is not a luxury for the few; it is not just for some people. It is meant for you and for me and for all of us. It is a simple duty, because if we learn to love, we learn to be holy.

MOTHER TERESA

Holiness is an infinite compassion for others.

RALPH IRON

What is a saint? It's someone who believes that God loves him.

LOUIS EVELY

A saint is simply a human being whose soul has . . . grown up to its full stature, by full and generous response to its environment, God. He has achieved a deeper, bigger life than the rest of us, a more wonderful contact with the mysteries of the Universe; a life of infinite possibility, the term of which he never feels that he has reached.

EVELYN UNDERHILL

The wonderful thing about saints is that they were *human*. They lost their tempers, got hungry, scolded God, were egotistical or testy or impatient in their turns, made mistakes and regretted them. Still they went on doggedly blundering toward heaven.

PHYLLIS MCGINLEY

Those we call saints rebelled against an outmoded and inadequate form of God on the basis of their new insights into divinity. . . . The continuous emergence of the God beyond God is the mark of creative courage in the religious sphere.

Rollo May

I am convinced that most of the saints were religious dropouts from societies that were going nowhere. Faith called them to drop out and believe in something else.

Richard Rohr

Saints are non-conformists.

Eleanor Ross Taylor

CTIONS

In our era, the road to holiness necessarily passes through the world of action.

DAG HAMMARSKJÖLD

We are not punished for our sins, but by them.

ELBERT HUBBARD

All our acts have sacramental possibilities.

FREYA STARK

Act, and God will act.

JOAN OF ARC

For us, there is only the trying. The rest is not our business.

T.S. ELIOT

It is the greatest of all mistakes to do nothing because you can only do little—*Do what you can.*

SYDNEY SMITH

The dramatic action that we need to create a way of life on Earth that really works will be taken not through personal, social, or political action, but through spiritual action.

BROOKE MEDICINE EAGLE

The "kingdom of heaven is within," indeed, but we must also create one without, because we are *intended* to act upon our circumstances.

FLORENCE NIGHTINGALE

All false religion proceeds in a certain sense from one illusion: People say, "Thy Kingdom come" out of one side of their mouth, but they don't, out of the other side of their mouth, say, "My kingdom go."

RICHARD ROHR

We are afraid of religion because it interprets rather than just observes. Religion does not confirm that there are hungry people in the world; it interprets the hungry to be our brethren whom we allow to starve.

DOROTHEE SÖLLE

There's only one way for God to distribute bread to those who lack it, and that's for us to give them ours.

LOUIS EVELY

God depends on us. It is through us that God is achieved.

ANDRÉ GIDE

God is no White Knight who charges into the world to pluck us like distressed damsels from the jaws of dragons, or diseases. God chooses to become present to and through us. It is up to us to rescue one another.

NANCY MAIRS

God has no other hands than ours.

DOROTHEE SÖLLE

 RELIGION

Religion is not an option or a strictly individual intuition, but represents the long unfolding, the collective experience of all mankind, of the existence of God.

TEILHARD DE CHARDIN

Religion in the life of man is a momentary glance from time into eternity.

THOMAS S. KEPLER

Religion . . . is a man's total reaction upon life.

WILLIAM JAMES

What is religion, you might ask. It's a technology of living.

TONI CADE BAMBARA

If we traverse the world, it is possible to find cities without walls, without letters, without wealth, without coin, without schools or theaters: but a city without a temple, or that practices not worship, prayers and the like, no one has ever seen.

PLUTARCH

Religion is as big as life and as normal an experience as breathing, eating, and sleeping.

THOMAS S. KEPLER

A little philosophy inclineth man's mind to atheism; but depth in philosophy bringeth men's minds about to religion.

FRANCIS BACON

Religion is probably, after sex, the second oldest resource which human beings have available to them for blowing their minds.

SUSAN SONTAG

You think religion is what's inside a little building filled with pretty lights from stained glass windows! But it's not. It's wings! *Wings!*

DOROTHY CANFIELD FISHER

"Religion" can no more be equated with what goes on in churches than "education" can be reduced to what happens in schools or "health care" restricted to what doctors do to patients in clinics. The vast majority of healing and learning goes on among parents and children and families and friends, far from the portals of any school or hospital. The same is true for religion. It is going on around us all the time. Religion is larger and more pervasive than churches.

HARVEY COX

The place of the church is not to change society, but to change men and women who will then do the changing of society.

DANIEL A. POLING

Religion was her theater, her dance, her wine, her song.

MERIDEL LE SUEUR

Religion was their meat and their excitement, their mental food and their emotional pleasure.

PEARL S. BUCK

When I speak of religion I mean a constant inward sense of communion with God.

RACHEL SIMON

Religion is a bridge to the spiritual, but the spiritual lies beyond religion.

RACHEL NAOMI REMEN

The world of religion is no longer a concrete fact proposed for our acceptance and adoration. It is an unfathomable universe which engulfs us, and which lives its own majestic uncomprehended life: and we discover that our careful maps and cherished definitions bear little relation to its unmeasured reality.

EVELYN UNDERHILL

This is what I found out about religion: it gives you courage to make the decisions you must make in a crisis and the confidence to leave the results to a higher Power. Only by trust in God can a man carrying responsibility find repose.

DWIGHT D. EISENHOWER

You have control over action alone, never over its fruits. Live not for the fruits of action, nor attach yourself to inaction.

THE BHAGAVAD-GITA

Reason does not get one far toward religion, but as far as it goes, it is indispensable.

GEORGIA HARKNESS

If we submit everything to reason, our religion will have no mysterious and supernatural element. If we offend the principles of reason, our religion will be absurd and ridiculous.

BLAISE PASCAL

Religion is an experience of God. Theology is merely an attempt to explain the experience.

AGNES SANFORD

Religion is different from everything else; *because in religion seeking is finding.*

WILLA CATHER

Too many people think religion consists
in what they do for God—
those poor, puny, pitiful things
they sometimes manage to do for Him.
Consequently, they find all of religion
poor, puny and pitiful
and they trudge along joylessly . . .
But religion consists
in what God does for us—
those great, stupendous things
He dreams up for us.

LOUIS EVELY

Religion without joy—it is no religion.

THEODORE PARKER

Religion is like music, one must have an ear for it. Some people have none at all.

CHARLOTTE MEW

Religion is caught, not taught.

WILLIAM R. INGE

Religion is love; in no case is it logic.

BEATRICE POTTER WEBB

Nothing is so deceptive as human reasoning,— nothing so slippery and reversible as what we have decided to call "logic." The truest compass of life is spiritual instinct.

MARIE CORELLI

Religion can't change the facts, but it can change the way you relate to facts.

HAROLD S. KUSHNER

A religious awakening which does not awaken the sleeper to love has roused him in vain.

JESSAMYN WEST

There is no religion without love, and people may talk as much as they like about their religion, but if it does not teach them to be good and kind to man and beast, it is all a sham.

ANNA SEWELL

Religion is the most widely debated and least agreed upon phenomenon of human history.

GEORGIA HARKNESS

Men who would persecute others for religious opinions, prove the errors of their own.

MARGUERITE BLESSINGTON

The historical religions have the tendency to become ends in themselves and, as it were, to put themselves in God's place, and, in fact, there is nothing that is so apt to obscure the face of God as a religion.

MARTIN BUBER

Our religious institutions have far too often become handmaidens of the status quo, while the genuine religious experience is anything but that. True religion is by nature disruptive of what has been, giving birth to the eternally new.

MARIANNE WILLIAMSON

Governments may change, and opinions, and the very appearance of lands themselves, but the slowest thing to change is religion. What has once been associated with worship becomes holy in itself, and self-perpetuating.

ELIZABETH COATSWORTH

Organized religious institutions are in for a huge transformation, for the simple reason that people have become genuinely religious in spite of them.

MARIANNE WILLIAMSON

I believe in God, only I spell it Nature.

FRANK LLOYD WRIGHT

When I am alone in the forest I always say my prayers; and that occasional solitary communion with God is surely the only true religion for intelligent beings.

GERTRUDE ATHERTON

Some keep the Sabbath going to church —
I keep it, staying at home —
With a bobolink for a chorister —
And an orchard, for a dome.

EMILY DICKINSON

Every day, people are straying away from the church and going back to God.

LENNY BRUCE

If absence makes the heart grow fonder, then a lot of folks sure do love the church.

MARTHA LUPTON

I am for religion, against religions.

VICTOR HUGO

It may be that religion is dead, and if it is, we had better know it and set ourselves to try to discover other sources of moral strength before it is too late.

PEARL S. BUCK

Nobody can deny but religion is a comfort to the distressed, a cordial to the sick, and sometimes a restraint on the wicked; therefore whoever would argue or laugh it out of the world without giving some equivalent for it ought to be treated as a common enemy.

LADY MARY WORTLEY MONTAGU

If I should go out of church whenever I hear a false sentiment I could never stay there five minutes. But why come out? The street is as false as the church.

RALPH WALDO EMERSON

If your religion is of the kind that can be easily hidden, it can be easily lost.

MARTHA LUPTON

If your religion does not change you, then you had better change your religion.

ELBERT HUBBARD

If you hold your religion lightly you are sure to let it slip.

MARTHA LUPTON

$\mathcal{M}$ANY WINDOWS

Let there be many windows to your soul . . .
Not the narrow pane
Of one poor creed can catch the radiant rays
That shine from countless sources.

ELLA WHEELER WILCOX

We're all moving in the same direction and that
direction is towards God, or Godhead, whatever you
want to call it.

SWAMI VISHNU-DEVANANDA

When souls before Thee reverently bow,
Oh, carest Thou what name the lips breathe low
Jove, or Osiris, or the God Unknown . . . ?

JULIA C.R. DORR

Say not, "I have found the truth," but rather, "I have found a truth."

Say not, "I have found the path of the soul." Say rather, "I have met the soul walking upon my path."

For the soul walks upon all paths.

The soul walks not upon a line, neither does it grow like a reed.

The soul unfolds itself, like a lotus of countless petals.

KAHLIL GIBRAN

Truth has never been, can never be, contained in any one creed or system!

MRS. HUMPHRY WARD

There is only one religion, though there are a hundred versions of it.

GEORGE BERNARD SHAW

All religions upon the earth are necessary because there are people who need what they teach. . . . Each church fulfills spiritual needs that perhaps others cannot fill. No one church can fulfill everybody's needs at every level.

BETTY J. EADIE

All denominations are needed—they fit a certain type of temperament. Down in Pennsylvania they break up the coal and send it tumbling through various sieves, and each size finds its place in a separate bin. If sects did not serve mankind they would never have been evolved—each sect catches a certain-sized man.

ELBERT HUBBARD

A thousand creeds have come and gone;
But what is that to you or me?
Creeds are but branches of a tree,
The root of love lives on and on.

ELLA WHEELER WILCOX

Sects are stoves, but fire keeps its old properties
through them all.

RALPH WALDO EMERSON

To know but one religion is not to know that one.
In fact superstition consists in this one thing—faith
in one religion, to the exclusion of all others.

ELBERT HUBBARD

Creeds grow so thick along the way,
Their boughs hide God; I cannot pray.

LIZETTE WOODWORTH REESE

Each drew his sword
On the side of the Lord.

PHYLLIS MCGINLEY

Great evil has been done on earth by people who think they have all the answers.

RUBY PLENTY CHIEFS

Spiritual wisdom is now available to everyone, disseminated to the masses as never before in world history. Finally, a few trips to the library, and we have a pretty good sense of what all the masters said. They all said the same things. There is a mass discovery that Jesus is truth, the Torah is truth, Muhammad is truth, Krishna is truth, Buddha is truth, and so on. They are all truth and they are all among us now.

MARIANNE WILLIAMSON

Those who enter heaven may find the outer walls plastered with creeds, but they won't find any on the inside.

JOSH BILLINGS

I am sort of a collector of religions, and the curious thing is I find I can believe in them all.

GEORGE BERNARD SHAW

Most philosophies wrap their seekers in a strict belief system. By virtue of what they include, they exclude everything else, especially some vital realizations. Periodically revising our philosophy of life as we live it is, therefore, a critically valuable exercise.

CHARLES BATES

There are many, many gates to the sacred and they are as wide as we need them to be.

SHERRY RUTH ANDERSON AND PATRICIA HOPKINS

There are many trails up the mountain, but in time they all reach the top.

ANYA SETON